Who Was Confucius?

by Michael Burgan

illustrated by Robert Squier

Penguin Workshop

For my friend and mentor, Teri Weidner.
You are missed by so many—RS

PENGUIN WORKSHOP
An Imprint of Penguin Random House LLC, New York

Published by Penguin Workshop, an imprint of Penguin Random House LLC, New York.
PENGUIN and PENGUIN WORKSHOP are trademarks of Penguin Books Ltd.
WHO HQ & Design is a registered trademark of Penguin Random House LLC.
Printed in the USA.

Visit us online at www.penguinrandomhouse.com.

Library of Congress Control Number: 2020033538

ISBN 9781524788735 (paperback) 10 9 8 7 6 5 4 3 2 1
ISBN 9781524788742 (library binding) 10 9 8 7 6 5 4 3 2 1

Contents

Who Was Confucius?

Some people in the city of Qufu might have been a little puzzled by the young boy named Kong Qiu. He lived there almost 2,600 years ago, and even then, children enjoyed playing with toys. Kong Qiu, though, was different. Starting at a very young age, he seemed to always consider the best way to behave. He also closely followed religious teachings and the traditions that went along with them. Kong Qiu was said to take dishes from his mother's kitchen and pretend they were the sacred bowls used in the religious ceremonies that he saw adults performing.

In Kong Qiu's time, Qufu was the capital of an independent state called Lu, one of many small states in what is now China. Across the country, people believed that they should honor their parents and the relatives who came before them. That belief was a main part of the religious traditions of the day.

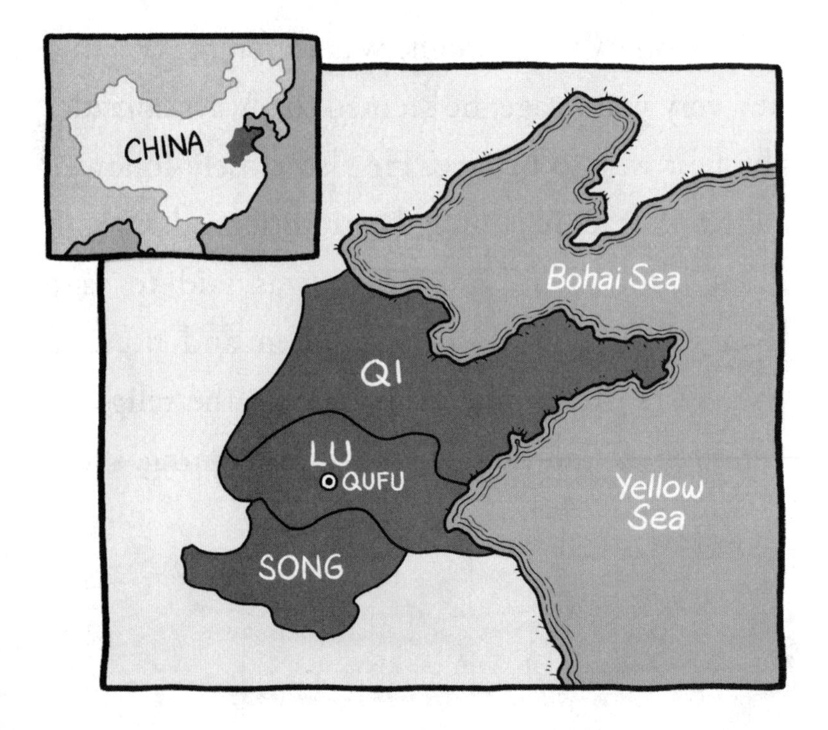

Like many children at that time, Kong Qiu began to learn all he could about the religious practices. He also learned songs that taught him about the plants and animals that were native to his region. Other songs described historical events or shared moral lessons. They helped Kong Qiu learn how to tell right from wrong. The boy believed he should always try to do what was right and speak up when others did something wrong. He thought everyone should behave this way.

As he grew older, Kong Qiu wanted to learn even more about religion, history, and how to behave in the most respectable way. He then set out to teach others about the importance of knowing right from wrong. He especially wanted to explain his beliefs to the rulers of the states around Lu. But as he did so, Kong Qiu learned that dukes and government officials of the smaller regions within the empire did not always want to listen to what he had to say! They often chose to do what was best for themselves instead of what was good for all their citizens.

Still, Kong Qiu found students who were eager to learn. They started to call him Kong Fuzi—that's Chinese for "Master Kong." His students later became teachers, too, and their students helped spread Kong Fuzi's teachings across China. Over the centuries, his ideas reached other parts of Asia as well.

Today, Kong Fuzi is also known as Confucius. He is considered one of the greatest thinkers and teachers ever. His ideas are rooted in the history of ancient China, but millions of people still embrace them as wise words. His teachings explain how to treat others well and live a good life.

CHAPTER 1
A Willing Student

Shuliang He Kong was a great warrior. Stories about his life say he was more than six feet tall, which would have made him seem like a giant in ancient China. He was also very strong. Once, he saved the lives of fellow soldiers by holding up a heavy gate that was about to trap the men inside an enemy castle. He was well-known in the state of Lu.

Shuliang He's family name was Kong, and his great-grandfather had come to Lu from the nearby state of Song. The Kongs had been a wealthy, well-respected family in Song, and some members held important positions in the government. But over time, they lost both their wealth and their power. For a time, Shuliang He held a minor government post in Lu, but his family did not have the privilege and respect the earlier Kongs did.

孔

Kong

Shuliang He had one son and nine daughters by his first wife. But as he got older, he decided he wanted to try to have a second son because his first son couldn't become his heir due to a foot problem. He married a second wife, named Zhengzai, and in 551 BCE, she did have a son. The baby had a bump on his head, so his mother named him Qiu (say: CHEW), which means "mound." In China, a person's family name comes first, so he was called Kong Qiu. His father's full name was actually Kong Shuliang He.

Kong Qiu was just three years old when his father died. Shuliang He didn't leave much money to Zhengzai and her son. Most of the little wealth the warrior had seemed to go to his first family.

The Mythical Birth of Confucius

Learning about Confucius's life is not easy. Most of the stories about his life were written hundreds of years after he died. In China, people wanted to show what a great man he was—and they weren't afraid to make up stories to "prove" it! Some stories about Confucius read like myths and legends. And some begin before he was even born!

One such story said that his mother, Zhengzai, dreamed of a unicorn while she was pregnant—a sign that her child would grow up to be an important person. Another myth said that two dragons guarded the spot where Zhengzai gave birth to Confucius, and then water miraculously sprang up from the ground. After Zhengzai bathed her son in the water, it all magically disappeared.

So the young boy with ties to what was once a powerful family faced a difficult childhood. He and his mother struggled to survive. But Zhengzai made sure that Kong Qiu learned all the important religious customs, especially the need to honor his father and other relatives who had died.

Besides what he learned from his mother, Kong Qiu may have taken classes at a local school. But he wanted to know even more. When he was older, he wrote, "At fifteen I set my heart on learning." He thought people needed an education. But Confucius didn't think people should boast about how smart they were. He felt they should take what they learned and help those in need.

Early Religious Beliefs

When Kong Qiu was born, China's main religious beliefs were already more than one thousand years old. The Chinese first believed that a god named Shangdi ruled over Earth. He was said to control the weather and choose who would win battles. Rulers made sacrifices of food or animals to win Shangdi's help. Later, the Chinese replaced the idea of this almighty god with the word *tian*, or "heaven." Tian was thought to influence life on Earth.

Shangdi

The Chinese also believed in ancestor worship. They honored the spirits of their dead relatives by making sacrifices for them. They also placed gifts at their graves. The spirits who were honored properly could bring good fortune to the living. Those who were not might haunt their living family members.

Religious teachings stressed treating family members well while they were alive, too. Children, in particular, were supposed to obey their parents and take care of them into their old age. Those ideas became a key part of Confucius's teaching.

Kong Qiu never described his education in detail, but he certainly read about the history of earlier Chinese rulers. Some five hundred years before Kong Qiu was born, the Zhou family established an empire in eastern China, near the Wei River. The Zhou emperors believed that heavenly powers shaped the universe and had chosen them to rule. This idea was called the Mandate of Heaven. Over the centuries,

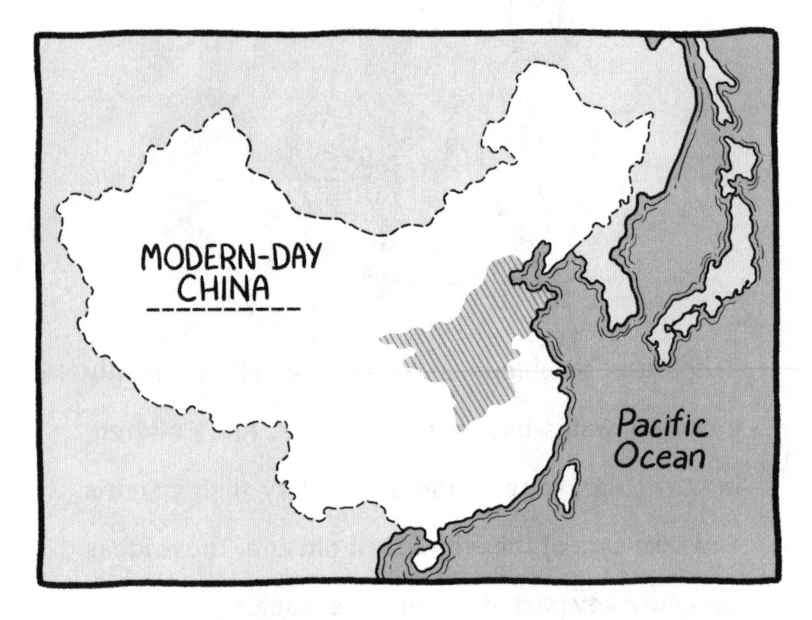

Zhou territory 1046–771 BCE

however, the Zhou family's power began to weaken. By around 771 BCE, the Zhou capital had moved east, to what is now China's Henan Province.

While the Zhou rulers still claimed the Mandate of Heaven, some of the more important families who were supposed to be loyal to them sought greater independence. And sometimes the heads of those families, who had the title of "duke,"

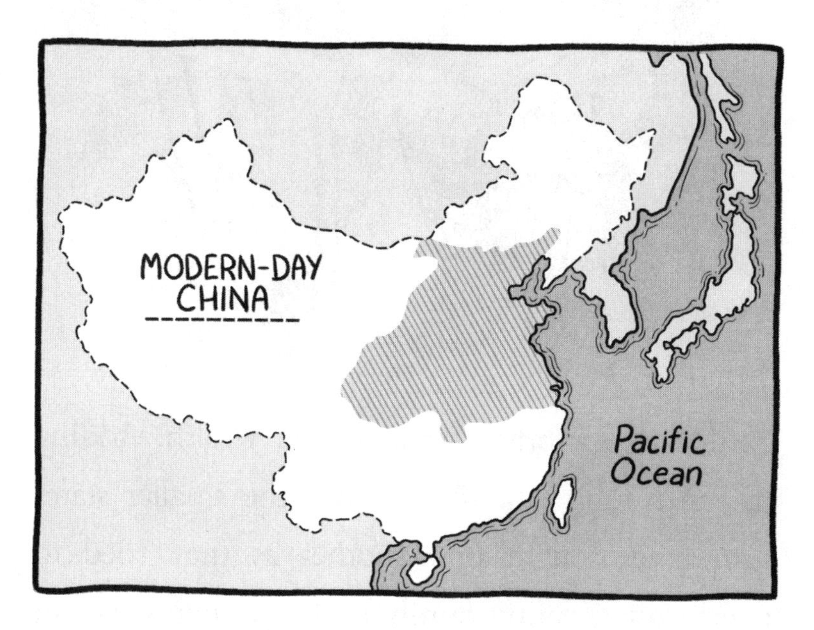

Zhou territory 770–256 BCE

battled one another for land and wealth. Adding to the troubles, families within the smaller states sometimes fought one another as they tried to overthrow a ruling family and put themselves in

power. Because of these warring dukes, Kong Qiu grew up in a time of great conflict and uncertainty. Before and during his life, about fifty small states were taken over by their more powerful neighbors.

Kong Qiu was a good student who knew what was happening in the lands around Lu. And his studies of history showed him that China had been much more peaceful when the Zhou emperors lived in the west and commanded loyalty from the dukes. Kong Qiu believed that those early emperors had been wise men who upheld the religious rites and tried to help their people. The emperors at that time were smart enough to listen to educated advisers, who helped shape their policies. The young scholar thought the rulers of his day should act like the old emperors had. And he believed that he could become a skilled and trusted adviser who would help the rulers do what was best for their lands and their people.

The first Zhou emperor, King Wu (in power from 1046 to 1043 BCE)

When he was nineteen, Kong Qiu was married. Within several years, he and his wife had a son, and the news of the child's birth reached Duke Zhao, the ruler of Lu. He probably knew that the Kong family had once been important, even if Kong Qiu had grown up poor. According to some stories, the duke presented Kong Qiu and his wife a gift of two carp—a type of fish.

After receiving the duke's gift, Kong Qiu named his son Li, the Chinese word for "carp." He was later known as Boyu, which means "top fish." Kong Qiu and his wife eventually had two daughters as well.

With his growing family, Kong Qiu had to stop his studies for a time and look for work. While he hoped one day he would be a trusted adviser to royal rulers, his first job was not so grand.

The Role of Women in Ancient China

The names of Confucius's wife and daughters are not found in any records. That may be because in ancient China, women were much lower in status than men. Most women were expected to stay at home and raise children. They could not inherit property from their fathers. But some women from royal families were exceptions.

Before the Zhou family came to power, a woman named Fu Hao was a fierce military commander. She was also allowed to take part in religious traditions that were usually only for men. Confucius, though, seemed to accept the idea that women's roles were mainly as wives and mothers.

Fu Hao

CHAPTER 2
Finding Work

As an adult, Kong Qiu was tall, like his father, but he had no interest in becoming a soldier. Instead, he hoped to find a government job, work hard, and use his knowledge to help others. But a young man from a poor family couldn't hope to start off in an important position. Government jobs were often given to the sons of wealthy families, even if they were not as bright as Kong Qiu. When he was offered a job with the Jisun family, one of the most important in Lu, Kong Qiu was glad to take it.

Kong Qiu recorded how much grain came into the Jisun warehouses and how much went out again. Along with recording how much grain was on hand, Kong Qiu had to make sure that insects or mice didn't infest the warehouses and eat the crops. People stored their grain, after crops were harvested, to have it all year long.

Kong Qiu did his job well, and soon he received a promotion. He was put in charge of the wealthy family's farm animals. He took his new job seriously, too. He said, "The oxen and sheep must be fat and strong and superior. That is all I have to care about."

But outside of work, Kong Qiu did care about other things, especially making sure he carried out all the religious customs that dated back to the time of the Zhou. When his mother, Zhengzai, died around 527 BCE, he arranged for her funeral. His father had been buried east of Lu, though Kong Qiu didn't know where. After he finally found the spot, he removed his mother's body from her original grave and buried her again beside his father. He then mourned her death for three years, according to the traditions.

Honoring the Dead

For the ancient Chinese, honoring their dead relatives was one of the most important religious customs. While in mourning, people typically did not wear their nicest clothes. Instead, they wore items made of rough cloth. They avoided fancy foods and didn't listen to music. Confucius believed that children should show deep grief when their parents died. This mourning period lasted for three years, since infants and toddlers rely on their parents so much during the first three years of their lives.

Confucius believed in honoring dead animals, too. When his dog died, he insisted that the pet be wrapped in cloth, as part of a proper burial.

Typical mourning dress included
white linen or sackcloth and a black armband

By the time of Zhengzai's death, Kong Qiu had begun to earn extra money as a teacher. He was already known for his great knowledge of the many songs and poems that explained Chinese history and the proper way to behave. Young men who did not come from powerful

or wealthy families hoped Kong Qiu would teach them these things so they could get good government jobs. He became a master to his students. Then Kong Qiu was called Kong Fuzi, which led to the name we know as "Confucius" today.

Confucius wanted each of his students to become a *junzi*—a word that means "gentleman" and usually describes men from wealthy families. But for Confucius, it meant much more than having a successful father or grandfather. A true *junzi* had to know and follow the religious rituals and treat others kindly. Confucius didn't care how much or how little money his students had—he would take as pay whatever they could afford. All he wanted was students who were eager to learn.

One of his first students, though, seemed to present a challenge. Zilu had come to Qufu from a family who lived in the countryside. He had a quick temper, and he and Confucius often argued with each other during the many years they spent together. When they first met, Zilu was said

Zilu

to have bragged about his long sword. Confucius asked him what good was having a weapon if he didn't have an education. Confucius learned that Zilu had plenty of courage, but he needed to learn how to act wisely.

Another of the master's early students was Yan Hui. Like Zilu, he was poor, but unlike the boastful farmer, Yan Hui was calm. More importantly, he readily understood all of Confucius's teachings. Still, he doubted he could ever match Confucius's knowledge and gentlemanly manners.

Yan Hui

Confucius was always learning new things, even as he taught others, and he was still working for the Jisuns. He was particularly interested in learning to play instruments. He loved music, especially older music from the Zhou Empire. He enjoyed the way musicians worked together to create something beautiful and how a tune flowed from beginning to end.

He also studied the way politicians interacted in the states around Lu. That way, he could offer advice to Duke Zhao if Confucius was ever asked for it.

For many years, Confucius continued to work for the Jisun family as he took on more students. Two were sons of the head of the Mengsuns, another important family in Lu. Because of his work for that family, Confucius's fame spread. By now, even Duke Zhao had heard of the work he was doing. As he approached forty, Confucius was at last offered a job by a powerful ruler.

CHAPTER 3
Success in Government

In his first job for Duke Zhao, Confucius was named the minister of works. He supervised public building projects, such as the construction of roads and bridges. Then, around 509 BCE, he was named the minister of crime. Confucius enforced the laws of Lu and made sure criminals were punished.

The ancient historians disagree about how well Confucius carried out this important job. Mencius, who lived in the fourth century BCE, said that the duke of Lu did not always follow Confucius's suggestions. But Sima Qian, who

lived over a hundred years after Mencius, claimed that Confucius quickly succeeded in making Lu a safer and better place to live.

Around the time Confucius became the minister of crime, a new duke came to power in Lu. This man, Duke Ding, thought well enough of Confucius to ask him to go on an important journey. In 500 BCE, Ding wanted to improve relations with the neighboring state of Qi (say: CHEE). The two states had fought each other at various times over the previous decades. Because of Confucius's knowledge of how to follow the ancient rules and act properly in all occasions, Ding brought him along on this important diplomatic mission.

Some ancient writings suggest that this journey with the duke was not Confucius's first trip to Qi. In 517 BCE, Duke Zhao of Lu had fled to Qi when the three most powerful families in the state rebelled against him.

A Famous Follower

Of all the scholars who studied with Confucius and the men who later passed on his teachings, Mencius is the most famous. He was born about one hundred years after Confucius lived. Like Confucius, Mencius was raised by a poor single mother who wanted her son to get a good education. Since she couldn't afford to pay for schooling, she had Mencius sit outside an open window by the local school so he could hear the teacher talk about Confucius's ideas. And like Confucius, Mencius wanted to help rulers achieve peace and treat their citizens well.

Mencius added one important idea to the teachings of Confucius: He believed people were not evil by nature, and they all have a deep inner belief that others shouldn't suffer. Like Confucius, he believed education was the key to proper behavior and feelings of goodwill among people. His own writings later helped spread Confucius's ideas.

By some accounts, Confucius and some of his students followed the duke to the neighboring land. It's most likely, though, that Confucius was still working for the Jisun family at the time and did not travel to Qi at that earlier date.

But at some point, certainly on his mission with Duke Ding, Confucius did meet Qi's Duke Jing. The *Analects*, a collection of Confucius's sayings and stories about his life, tells of several conversations he had with the foreign duke. In one conversation, Jing asked Confucius about the best way to rule. "Let a ruler be a ruler," he said, "a subject a subject, a father a father, a son a son."

Confucius meant that everyone had a certain role to play in society, and they should do everything that was expected of them. For rulers, that didn't mean they had total power to do what they wanted. They should try to keep peace

and make sure basic needs, like food and housing, were met. The subjects were the common people who were dependent on the noble families. In return, they were under the nobles' control.

Chinese Writing

The Chinese developed a system of writing about five thousand years ago. Instead of using letters, as in the English alphabet, the Chinese developed a character-based writing system. One character might represent an entire word or a few words that form a phrase. Some of China's earliest rulers wrote on bones. Later, educated officials working for the rulers wrote on pieces of silk, bamboo, or wood. They used brushes dipped in ink to create the characters. The Chinese eventually invented paper (about six hundred years after Confucius lived).

Ancient Chinese texts were read from right to left. The characters were written in columns, with a sentence starting at the top and going down. Today, written Chinese has close to fifty thousand characters, but most people use only about four thousand to five thousand.

The subjects were expected to obey the laws of the land and pay their taxes. They also had a duty to teach their children morals. And children had the duty of obeying their parents while they were alive and honoring them after they died. These were some of Confucius's key beliefs.

And the noble families were impressed by these ideas. They wanted their subjects to be as loyal to them as children were to their parents.

But while Confucius and Duke Jing had some pleasant conversations, the duke of Qi had more on his mind than making peace with Lu. He actually wanted to use the meeting with Duke Ding to kidnap him! Before leaving Lu, Confucius had a hunch that Duke Jing might try to harm the members of Lu's peace party. He had told his duke to make sure he brought soldiers with him. As usual, he relied on history as a guide.

The Sayings of Confucius

The *Analects* provides a useful account of Confucius's life and ideas. The title means "brief sayings," and Confucius is sometimes called the author of the book, but that's not true. No one knows exactly who collected his sayings and the stories that are told in the *Analects*. What's clear, though, is that some students of Confucius and later teachers wrote different parts of the book. Some sections were written long after Confucius died.

The *Analects* is divided into twenty parts, often called books, and each book has a number of short entries—some just a few words long. The book also names some of Confucius's students, as well as the people he met during his travels.

He told Duke Ding that in centuries past, rulers never left their own lands without soldiers to protect them.

The two dukes held their meeting in the valley of Xiagu (say: SHAG-u) in Qi. Duke Jing had recruited warriors from outside his state to carry out the kidnapping. But before they could spring into action, Confucius sensed that something was wrong, and he called for the soldiers from Lu to step forward. Then Confucius addressed Duke Jing and told him that trying to use force against Duke Ding was wrong.

The duke of Qi realized that Confucius was right. He ordered the foreign soldiers to leave, and the meeting went on as planned. The duke of Lu received his major demand—the return of three cities that Qi had captured earlier.

The meeting in Xiagu was the brightest spot in Confucius's career in government. Most likely, he had saved his ruler's life. He certainly had negotiated favorable terms for Lu in the treaty signed there. And, once again,

he had been clever enough to illustrate the best way to find a solution: by doing the right thing. But when he returned to Lu, trouble was brewing in his homeland.

CHAPTER 4
Difficult Times

Almost one hundred years before Confucius was born, three powerful families began to emerge in Lu. In theory, they were supposed to be loyal to the duke, just as the duke was supposed to be loyal to the emperor. But the Three Families of Lu all did whatever served their interests. These families—the Jisuns, Shusuns, and Mengsuns—had their own private armies, and they weren't afraid to use them to challenge the duke.

Confucius had seen that the power of the Three Families threatened the duke's ability to keep order in Lu. He knew about the rebellion that had forced Duke Zhao to flee Lu in 517 BCE. Now, since Confucius worked for Duke

Ding, he wanted to make sure that the Three Families did not weaken the duke's power.

Along with their own armies, the Three Families also had large castles. In 498 BCE, Confucius convinced Duke Ding that only he should have strong walled cities to protect him from attack. And Confucius knew there were people in Lu who hated both the three powerful clans and Duke Ding. Confucius feared that these rebels, who were not loyal to any single family, could seize one of the families' castles and use it as a base to launch an all-out war.

Duke Ding followed Confucius's advice and told the Three Families that they should tear down their castles. Confucius's student Zilu was working for the Jisun family, and he encouraged the heads of all the families to follow Ding's order. The Shusuns did as they were told.

The Jisuns were ready to dismantle their castle, too, in the city of Bi. But Gongshan Furao, who also worked for the Jisun family, wanted to resist the order. He put together a rebel army in Bi and took control of the castle. He also reached out to Confucius, asking him to join him in Bi.

According to the *Analects*, Zilu was surprised that Confucius would even think of meeting with a rebel. All of the master's teachings stressed preserving order and obeying the law. Confucius, however, thought that perhaps he could help Gongshan Furao be a wise and fair ruler, like the old Zhou emperors. But in the end, Confucius remained loyal to Duke Ding.

From Bi, Gongshan Furao led his rebels to Qufu, the capital of Lu. Duke Ding and the heads of the Three Families fled to a palace, running up a tower to avoid the invaders. As enemy arrows whizzed by the tower, Confucius took action. He ordered several military officers to lead a counterattack against the rebels. The duke's soldiers drove Gongshan Furao and his men out of Qufu and defeated them outside the city. The Jisun family then destroyed its castle.

The third family, the Mengsuns, still resisted Duke Ding's order to destroy their castle. The duke led an army against it, but he could not defeat the Mengsuns' army. He returned to Qufu in defeat.

Recording the History of Lu

Information about the rebellion in Lu during Confucius's life comes mostly from two books. One is the *Spring and Autumn Annals*, which Lu officials used to record important yearly political events. It's considered China's first history book.

This record was begun in 722 BCE and kept for almost 250 years. The name suggests the passing of one year, even though only two of the four seasons are named. The era in Chinese history that began around 770 BCE and ended around 476 BCE is called the Spring and Autumn Period, named after this important book. The entries in the annals, which are the historical records for each year, are often short. They might list simply one month and an event such as a religious ceremony or a natural disaster.

More details about these events were written in later books called commentaries. One of the most important is the *Zuo Commentary*. It was written between 400 and 300 BCE. This book tells the story of the battle that raged in Qufu in 498 BCE.

Duke Ding seemed to lose respect for Confucius in the time after the rebellion. Although Confucius had called out to soldiers to defend the duke, he had also come up with the idea of destroying the castles—the plan that had sparked the rebellion in the first place. Jihuanzi, the duke's top adviser, also seemed to think less of Confucius after what happened in 498 BCE. Jihuanzi was part of the Jisun clan,

and perhaps he didn't like that Confucius was trying to weaken the power of the Three Families.

In 497 BCE, the duke of Qi sent Duke Ding a gift of sixty horses. Beautiful dancing women arrived along with the animals. Jihuanzi convinced Duke Ding that they should watch the women dance, and the two men forgot about their government work for three days.

Confucius was upset that such important men would ignore their duties simply to be entertained.

Then, Duke Ding held an official sacrifice of an animal. These sacrifices were part of religious ceremonies meant to honor dead ancestors as well as spirits that lived in heaven and on Earth. As a government official, Confucius should have received some of the roasted meat from the animal killed for the sacrifice. But the duke didn't offer any to Confucius.

Both Jihuanzi and the duke had offended Confucius. He decided it was time to leave Lu. Mencius later guessed that Confucius had been thinking of leaving Lu even before he was treated so rudely at the sacrificial meal. He may have already realized that Ding and Jihuanzi had lost their trust in him. But watching Duke Ding not follow the traditions properly gave Confucius a good excuse to leave his homeland. Many years would pass before he returned.

CHAPTER 5
The Wanderer

Zilu, Yan Hui, and several of Confucius's other favorite students went with him when he left Lu. Some of those men were making great sacrifices to travel with their master, since they had jobs and families in Lu. At age fifty-four,

Confucius no longer had family responsibilities. He was divorced, and his children were now adults. Although the route they took is not clear, Confucius did make stops in at least six Chinese states outside his homeland.

The group's first stop was Wei, a small state about 120 miles from Qufu. From his studies, Confucius knew that Wei's rulers had a history of using skilled advisers. Perhaps the current duke, named Ling, would have use for Confucius's skills.

But even after Confucius spent almost a year in Wei, the duke never offered him a job. Confucius then headed for Jin. It had been one of the most powerful states during the Spring and Autumn Period, but war between different families was beginning to weaken the region. Before Confucius entered Jin, he learned that a powerful family there was planning to rebel against the duke. Confucius decided to avoid Jin and headed back to Wei.

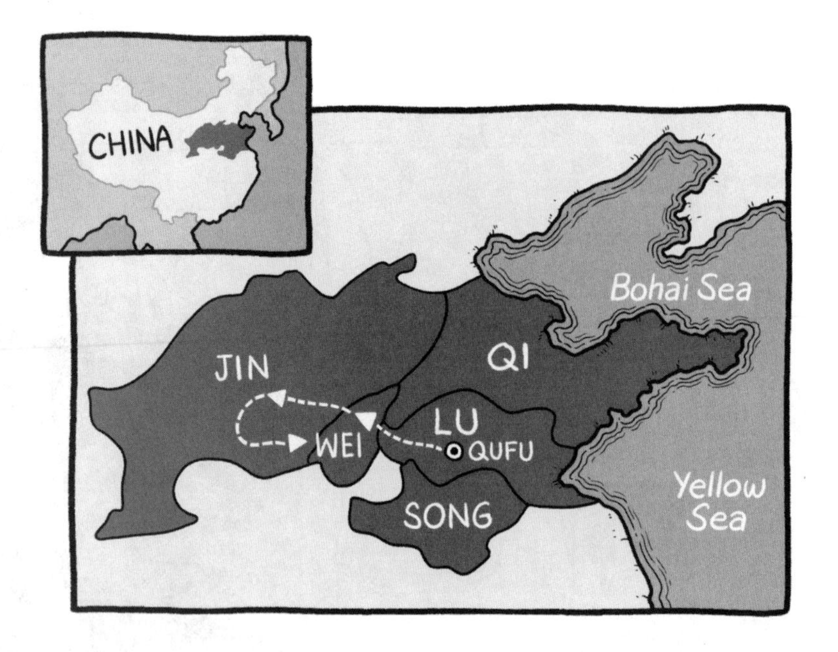

Confucius finally went to work for Duke Ling, though his position was not clear. The *Analects* reports just one meeting between the two men. Duke Ling asked Confucius a question about how to use his military. Confucius said he knew plenty about religious practices but little about warfare. Confucius thought the duke was more interested in fighting, as well as his own pleasure, than in ruling well. Ling died in 493 BCE, and Confucius and his students left Wei in search of another ruler to advise.

The group headed next for Song, the homeland of Confucius's ancestors. But he didn't receive a very warm greeting there—in fact, a man named Huan Tui tried to kill him! Huan Tui was an important government official in Song. According to one ancient source, Huan Tui tried a very odd method to get rid of Confucius: He ordered men to cut down a tree that Confucius and his students were standing underneath.

The plot failed, and Confucius believed that heaven had protected him because he was a good man.

In the city of Kuang in the state of Zheng, Confucius escaped death a second time. An angry mob gathered around him. They mistook him for a foreign leader who had captured some citizens of Kuang several years before. Confucius looked like their enemy, but he was able to convince the mob that he was not the man they wanted to kill.

In 492 BCE, the men arrived in the state of Chen. After three years there, with Confucius never finding a job, they ran out of food and came close to starving. The *Analects* says that the men "fell so ill that none could rise from bed." Zilu asked Confucius why the *junzi*—well-mannered gentlemen—would be facing starvation. Confucius replied that gentlemen could survive any problem they faced.

Confucius was right. He and his students did survive. But at some point during his time in Chen, Confucius became homesick. He called out to his students, "Let us return, let us return!"

He thought those who had still remained in Lu would welcome more of his teachings. But he and his followers did not go home.

The group ended up in the state of Chu, in a region called She. The governor of She asked for Confucius's advice on the best way to rule. Confucius did not tell him specific details about what to do. But he thought that—generally speaking—the governor should rule in such a way that people living in his region would want to stay there. And if he ruled well, people from far away would want to move there.

Confucius probably left She around 487 BCE. He and his students had been traveling for ten long years. Confucius decided it was time to stop wandering. They began to head north, making the long journey back to Lu.

Confucius and the Golden Rule

Some five hundred years or so after Confucius lived, the Bible set down these words of Jesus Christ: "In everything, do to others as you would have them do to you." Those words are now known as the "golden rule," and Confucius had his own version of it.

Speaking to his student Zhonggong, he said, "Do not do to others what you would not wish done to you. Then there can be no complaint against you." Another time, when his student Zigong asked for just one sentence to describe how people should act, Confucius said, "That which you do not desire, do not do to others." Around the world, people of many different religions follow their own version of the golden rule.

Zigong

CHAPTER 6
Coming Home

While Confucius was making his way back home, some of his students were hard at work. They had found government jobs in different states, including Lu.

One, Ran Qiu, had become a top adviser to the Jisun family in Lu. Another, Zidong, was highly regarded in that state for his knowledge of religious customs and traditions—knowledge he had learned from Confucius.

Ran Qiu

Ran Qiu worked to boost his reputation in spring 484 BCE. That year, troops from the state of Qi threatened Lu. Ran Qiu encouraged the Jisun family to prepare for war. When the enemy attacked, Ran Qiu led the defense and drove them off. That military success impressed the Jisun family and government leaders in Lu. Ran Qiu then convinced these important men to invite Confucius back to Lu. Soon, Confucius received a note from the head of the Jisun family and Lu's new duke, named Ai. They promised to pay him if he came home. Confucius accepted the invitation and was back home before the end of the year.

Although he had not become the most well-known adviser, Confucius did have a good reputation in Lu. Now in his midsixties, he found that young men were eager to become his students. Duke Ai considered him a state's elder—someone who was respected for the wisdom he had acquired over a long life.

Lu was once again facing difficult times. The Three Families still held great power and wealth. And the Jisun clan hoped to grow their fortune. The family proposed collecting a new tax from the common people who farmed land that belonged to the Jisuns. And the Jisuns owned more land in Lu than any other family. Ran Qiu asked Confucius what he thought of the idea, and at first, Confucius simply said he didn't know anything about the issue. In reality, Confucius knew that Ran Qiu would not want to hear what he thought. Confucius realized that his former student and his bosses wanted the new tax. Confucius, however, thought it would hurt the farmers, who already paid other taxes. Finally, in a private conversation, Confucius told Ran Qiu that he thought the new tax was unfair.

Despite his teacher's opinion, in 483 BCE, Ran Qiu helped the Jisuns put the new land tax

in place. An angry Confucius told his students, “He is no follower of mine! Young men, you have my permission to . . . drive him away.”

To Confucius, Ran Qiu was the wrong kind of political adviser—he did what the important families wanted him to do, even if it could be harmful to others in their community. Confucius challenged Ran Qiu once again, when the former student told Confucius that the Jisuns wanted to attack a small neighboring state. Confucius said he opposed the invasion. Ran Qiu tried to make excuses for why it was the right thing to do, even though their neighbor was not a threat to the Lu region. Confucius said a *junzi* did not make excuses for doing something that was harmful to others.

Confucius saw that he couldn't influence his former student. And though Duke Ai and leaders of the Three Families sometimes spoke to Confucius, they rarely seemed to actually listen to him. Now in his late sixties, Confucius put more of his effort into teaching younger students. One was named Zizhang. He was one of the smartest of these new students. As recorded in the *Analects*, he asked Confucius

many questions about what was right and what was wrong. Later in the book, sayings from Zizhang are quoted as well. This young man didn't hide his desire to find a good, and high-paying, government job. Although Confucius thought that gentlemanly behavior was more important than money, he offered Zizhang advice about how to reach his goal. He told Zizhang to make as few mistakes as possible in what he said and did, and he would find a good job.

Confucius also kept up his own studies of history, poetry, and song. Over the years, he had come to love a form of music called *shao*. The songs were about an ancient emperor named Shun. The *Analects* says that when Confucius first heard *shao*, he considered it a perfect form of music. He was so thrilled by it, he barely tasted his food for three months. All he could think about was that beautiful music.

Chinese historians believe that Confucius also stayed busy writing. During his later years, he wrote or edited several important books, called the Five Classics. Although they are still linked to Confucius's thoughts, modern historians are not so sure that he actually wrote them.

The Five Classics

Five books associated with Confucius and his teachings influenced Chinese thought for centuries. They are:

Spring and Autumn Annals—a record of historical events in the Lu region.

Book of Changes—a book of history and inspiration that offers guidance by using random numbers. This book is also called the *I Ching*, and some people still use it.

Book of Rites—a record of rituals dating back to the Zhou dynasty.

Book of Odes (sometimes called the *Book of Songs*)—a collection of songs and poems.

Book of Documents—the history of some of ancient China's first kings and empires.

CHAPTER 7
Death of a Master

In 479 BCE, Confucius's student Zigong returned to Lu and visited his old teacher. He found the seventy-three-year-old Confucius holding a cane to help support his weight.

The old man paced back and forth in front of his home. He told Zigong about a dream he had just had. The dream, Confucius was sure, meant he would die soon. With tears in his eyes, he told Zigong that he feared his students would not pass on his teachings after he was gone.

Confucius's dream then seemed to come true. He became sick, and he died only a week after speaking to Zigong. One of his students made sure that Confucius was buried properly.

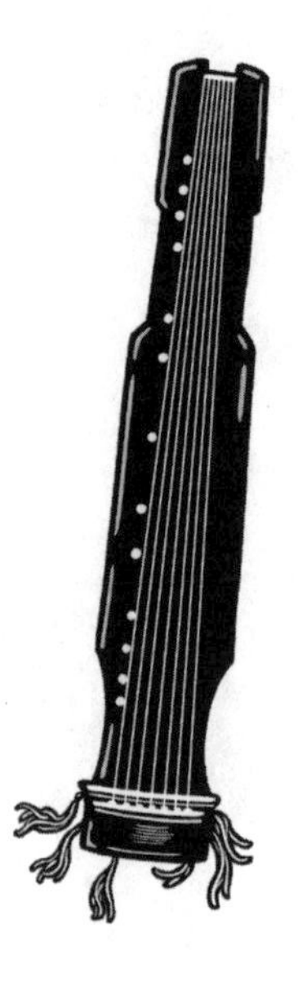

That included putting up fans that would shade the coffin from the sun and burying Confucius with items that he had used during his life. They may have included instruments he had played and books he had treasured. Confucius's students then mourned him for three years, the same way they would have honored their own parents.

Duke Ai mourned the master's death, too. He said that heaven was unkind because it had taken away such a great man. But Zigong questioned the duke's true feelings. He knew that when Confucius was alive, the duke had ignored his advice. It was wrong now, Zigong said, for Ai to praise him.

Confucius, it turns out, was wrong about one thing. His ideas about how to be a gentleman and live an honorable life were remembered long after his death. Some of his students took on their own students, so they could pass on Confucius's teachings. One even stayed in Lu to teach, and he is quoted several times in the *Analects* as Master Shen. He once said the heart of Confucius's teachings was loyalty and following the golden rule. One of Confucius's grandsons, named Zisi, was born just two or three years before Confucius died. He later became a Confucian teacher, too.

Zisi, grandson of Confucius

Some ancient historians claimed that Zisi eventually taught Mencius, who helped spread the Confucian ideas. In truth, Mencius most likely did not study with the master's grandson. But his writings about Confucius's life and teachings became an important part of the rules that future students studied.

In 221 BCE, after centuries of constant warfare among the different Chinese states, a man named Ying Zheng finally united China into a single empire. His advisers said the emperor had the power to use his military against his own people and to raise taxes.

Ying Zheng

And in a decision that would have horrified Confucius, the new emperor burned many books and even killed some scholars when their teachings went against government policies.

The new emperor's violent ways and thirst for complete power sparked a rebellion. In 202 BCE, a new emperor named Gaozu (say: GOW-zoo) took control of the government. He and the members of his family who ruled after him were much friendlier to Confucius's original teachings.

Confucian scholars ran many schools during this time, and they used the Five Classics associated with Confucius as some of their basic texts. Other books that students read included one by Mencius and *Doctrine of the Mean*, which may have been written by Confucius's grandson Zisi.

Emperor Gaozu was the founder of a ruling family known as the Han dynasty. Han was the name of a small state that Gaozu controlled before he became emperor of all of China. He founded what became the first long-lasting dynasty in the country. Except for a few short periods, the Han dynasty lasted for more than four hundred years. Under the Han emperors,

Emperor Gaozu

China began trading with lands in Central Asia, and Chinese goods eventually reached Europe as well. All types of products were carried along a route now called the Silk Road.

While the Han family ruled, one of its subjects invented paper, and the historian Sima Qian wrote the first history of the world as the Chinese knew and understood it at that time. He often mentioned Confucius in his writings. Today, people called Han Chinese are the largest ethnic group in China.

Papermaking during the Han dynasty

The Silk Road

An internationally important series of trade routes that stretched from China to the Mediterranean Sea and north through Europe, the Silk Road was originally a network established to trade jade and other goods. In 1877, it was given its current name because of the growing popularity of Chinese silk.

Silkworm cocoons

One of the most valuable products made in ancient China was silk cloth. It is made from the thread that silkworms spin to build their cocoons. During Confucius's life, only the Chinese knew how to make this prized fabric. To keep the secret, the emperors threatened to kill anyone who told a foreigner how to make it! But the Chinese did trade silk for other supplies.

Starting a little over two thousand years ago, the Chinese traded silk with Egypt and the Roman Empire. Traders followed a number of roads and rivers in Central Asia, moving by both boat and camel to exchange products, including gunpowder, and techniques, such as papermaking. The Chinese returned with horses, food, and items made of metal.

Before the end of the second century BCE, the ruling family decided that knowing the Five Classics was essential for getting a job in the government. Within roughly two centuries, thousands of students each year attended a university that taught Confucius's ideas. Teachers of other religions and schools of thought still tried to gain influence with the emperors. But Confucian ideas shaped China for centuries to come.

CHAPTER 8
One Man's Lasting Impact

Under the Han rulers, the influence of Confucius's thoughts continued to grow. The emperors liked his ideas. They felt that if rulers and their subjects followed set rules, there was little risk that the people would rebel. But the Confucian teachings also called on rulers, and everyone else, to treat others with respect. That idea was very strong within each family as well. The Chinese stressed the idea that children should honor and obey their parents.

Over time, more schools opened up in China to teach Confucian beliefs. After the end of the Han dynasty, the Sui dynasty required government workers not only to study the Five Classics but also to pass a test that proved their knowledge of them. Future emperors sometimes supported religions or belief systems other than Confucianism. But they never totally weakened the influence of Master Kong's ideas.

Over the centuries, China's influence in East Asia grew. Leaders in Korea, Japan, and Vietnam borrowed ideas from the Chinese about how to run a government. They also adopted Confucian teachings. By the twentieth century, though, many Chinese thinkers began to reject Confucius and his ideas. Scholars and political leaders thought they were old-fashioned. For a time in the 1960s and 1970s, students did not study the Five Classics at all, and the government banned his ideas.

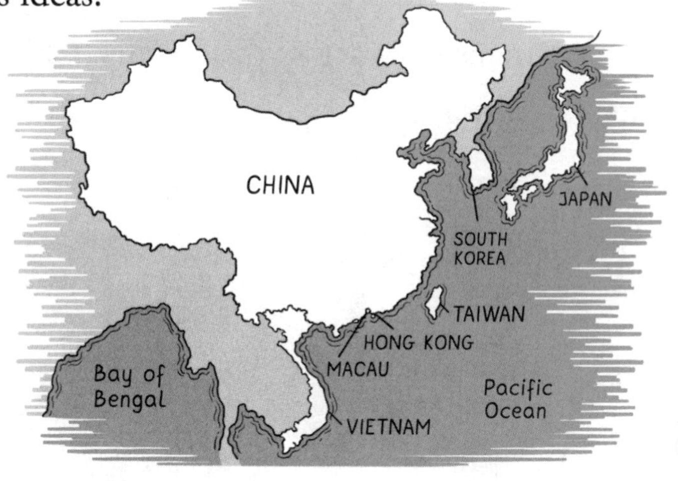

Countries where Confucianism is taught and followed

Today, though, leaders in China and other Asian countries once again see value in what Confucius had to say. Some business owners like the idea that people should treat one another with respect. They share Confucian teachings with their workers. And they believe that people should be hired for government jobs because of their knowledge, not because they come from powerful families.

China today is a modern nation of more than one billion people! Its cities are filled with skyscrapers. High-speed trains whiz across the country. Chinese businesses sell all kinds of products around the world.

The business district in Beijing

Confucius would not recognize this China. But he would probably be thrilled to see that his ideas about how to live a good life are still able to shape new ways of thinking and better ways of living.

Honoring Confucius

Some people have called Confucianism a religion. Confucius never made that claim, though he did base his philosophy—his way of thinking—on ancient religious beliefs. Confucius was more concerned with how people treated one another while they were alive than with talking about what happened after they died. But that didn't stop some later followers of his from honoring him as if he were a religious figure.

In Qufu, some people turned his former home into a temple, and they offered sacrifices to him, just as they would to heavenly spirits. Other towns built temples to honor him, too. Today, people flock to Qufu to visit the Confucian temple that still stands there. In Qufu, tourists can also see a brass statue of Confucius that is 236 feet tall. It's the tallest statue of him in the world. The New York City neighborhood of Chinatown also honors Master Kong with its own statue.

Temple of Confucius in Qufu

Timeline of Confucius's Life

551 BCE	Kong Qiu, later known as Confucius, is born in Qufu in the state of Lu
c. 533 BCE	Confucius marries
c. 527 BCE	His mother, Zhengzai, dies
c. 511 BCE	Named the minister of works in Lu
c. 509 BCE	Named the minister of crime in Lu
500 BCE	Duke Ding of Lu takes Confucius to the state of Qi, where Confucius saves the duke from a kidnapping
498 BCE	A rebellion breaks out in Lu, and Confucius orders soldiers to protect Duke Ding
497 BCE	With several of his students, leaves Lu and heads to the state of Wei
493 BCE	With his students, leaves Wei
c. 492 BCE	Survives an attempted murder in Song
	Reaches Chen with his students
489 BCE	While in Chen, Confucius and his students almost starve
484 BCE	Ran Qiu convinces the new duke of Lu to invite Confucius back to his homeland
	Returns to Lu
479 BCE	Dies in Qufu

Timeline of the World

c. 563 BCE	The Buddha, the founder of Buddhism, is born in what is now Nepal
518 BCE	Darius the Great of Persia begins building a new capital city, known today as Persepolis
509 BCE	The Roman Republic is founded
c. 500 BCE	The city of Monte Albán is founded in what is now Mexico
c. 490 BCE	The Greek mathematician Pythagoras dies
c. 486 BCE	The Chinese begin building a canal to connect the Yellow and Yangtze Rivers
250 BCE	The town of Djenné-Djeno in Mali, Africa, is founded and becomes a major trade center
221 BCE	Construction begins on the Great Wall of China
	The many Chinese states are united under a new emperor

Bibliography

***Books for young readers**

*Carew-Miller, Anna. ***Confucius: Great Chinese Philosopher***. Broomall, PA: Mason Crest, 2014.

Chin, Annping. ***The Authentic Confucius: A Life of Thought and Politics***. New York: Scribner, 2007.

Clements, Jonathan. ***Confucius: A Biography***. N.p.: Albert Bridge Books, 2017.

Confucius. ***The Analects***. Edited by Michael Nylan. Translated by Simon Leys. New York: W. W. Norton, 2014.

Confucius. ***The Analects***. Translated by Raymond Dawson. New York: Oxford University Press, 2008.

Confucius. ***The Analects of Confucius: An Online Teaching Translation***. Version 2.21. Translated by Robert Eno. IU ScholarWorks. 2015. https://scholarworks.iu.edu/dspace/handle/2022/23420.

*Faust, Daniel R. ***Ancient China***. New York: Gareth Stevens Publishing, 2019.

McArthur, Meher. ***Confucius: A Throneless King***. New York: Pegasus Books, 2011.

Riegel, Jeffrey. "Confucius." The Stanford Encyclopedia of Philosophy. https://plato.stanford.edu/entries/confucius/#ConEdu (accessed January 12, 2020).

Schuman, Michael. ***Confucius and the World He Created***. New York: Basic Books, 2015.